ALG

An Illustrated Poem

JAMES SAVAGE

NATURAL HERITAGE/NATURAL HISTORY INC.

Algonquin: An Illustrated Poem
Published by Natural Heritage/Natural History Inc.
P.O. Box 95, Station O
Toronto, Ontario M4A 2M8
© James Savage
All Rights Reserved

Design: Derek Chung Tiam Fook
Printed and bound in Canada by Hignell Printing Limited, Winnipeg, Manitoba
Typeset in Utopia and printed on Eco Matte Paper (recycled).
First Printing May 1993.

Canadian Cataloguing in Publication Data
Savage, James, 1908 –
         Algonquin: an illustrated poem

ISBN 0-920474-70-5
1. Algonquin Provincial Park (Ont.) – Poetry.
2. Algonquin Provincial Park (Ont.) – Pictorial works
I. Title

RS8587A82A8 1993 C811'.54 C92-093474-9
PR919.3.S28A8 1993

Front Cover:
Tom Thomson 1877-1917
Autumn, Algonquin Park c. 1915
oil on canvas
51.2 x 41.0 cm
McMichael Canadian Art Collection
Gift of Mr. C.F. Wood
1975.22

Dedicated to the memory of
two great biologists who were
my friends and teachers
Professor J. R. Dymond
and
Dr. William Harkness

" We cannot change yesterday.
We can only make the most of today.
and look with hope
toward tomorrow."

Dear Grandson

We love you.

Christmas 2013

God Bless

XO

Grandad a Grandma

"It is here that the imagination of the poet kindles into reverie and rapture, and revels in almost incommunicable luxury of thought."

Alexander Kirkwood,
in a letter to the
Hon. T.B. Pardee,
Commissioner of
Crown Lands, 1885

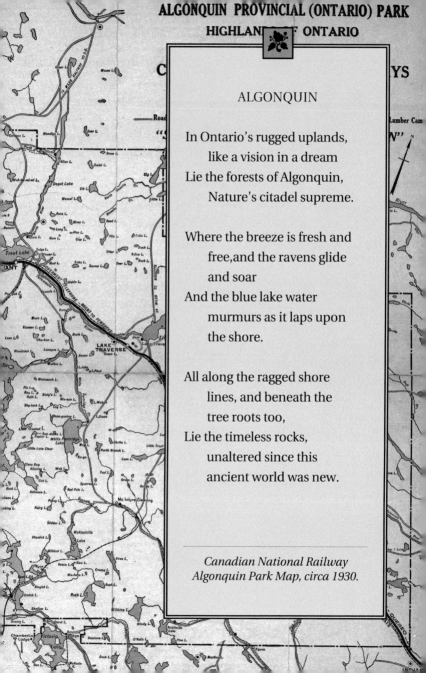

ALGONQUIN

In Ontario's rugged uplands,
　　like a vision in a dream
Lie the forests of Algonquin,
　　Nature's citadel supreme.

Where the breeze is fresh and
　　free, and the ravens glide
　　and soar
And the blue lake water
　　murmurs as it laps upon
　　the shore.

All along the ragged shore
　　lines, and beneath the
　　tree roots too,
Lie the timeless rocks,
　　unaltered since this
　　ancient world was new.

*Canadian National Railway
Algonquin Park Map, circa 1930.*

Its hills and dales were
    sculptured, in a cold and
    distant past,
By the chisel of the glaciers,
    irresistible and vast.

But when the sun regained its
    strength, it loosed the
    mighty vice,
With the softening of the
    climate, and the melting
    of the ice

Then the valleys, full of water,
    looked like strings of
    azure beads,
Where the feeding fish swam
    lazily among the rocks
    and reeds.

*The mystique of Algonquin waters
was captured by an early park
visitor in this previously
unpublished photograph.*

Soon leafy sylvan glory
    clothed the undulating
    hills,
And in beds of moss and fern
    glistened little ponds and
    rills.

Time's slow and silent
    passage wove its magic
    over all,
And Nature, uncontested,
    ruled her creatures great
    and small.

When many moons had
    come and gone at Time's
    unhurried pace,
A strange and startling thing
    appeared - a new and
    different race.

Algonquin, May, 1951.

On rock tree-clad headland
   there are wigwams...a
   canoe!
Where wisps of white and
   swirling smoke ascent
   toward the blue.

The braves are paddling off to
   fish, the women stay
   behind,
The baby sleeps in mossy bag
   that thread-like rootlets
   bind.

Behold the maid in doeskin
   cloak who moves with
   supple grace
To tend the fire, or weave a
   mat, or basket tightly
   lace.

The main water routes responded to
the touch of native paddlers when
Algonquin was a forest wilderness.

With joy and neat precision
    she adorns her garments
    fine,
All lovingly embroidered with
    the quill of porcupine.

These Indian Algonquins to
    this happy land lay claim,
And here they lived
    contentedly, and here
    they left their name.

Anon came other fiercer
    tribes, then peace and
    gladness waned,
And for a while, hate, stealth
    and guile, and fear and
    horror reigned.

A depiction of a native encampment by an unsigned artist, circa 1870-1880.

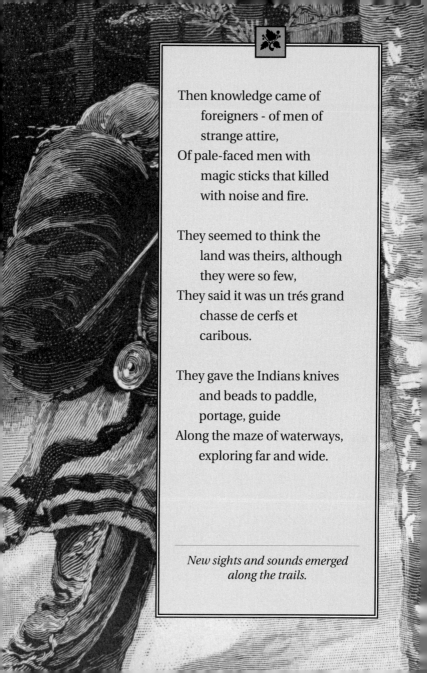

Then knowledge came of
	foreigners - of men of
	strange attire,
Of pale-faced men with
	magic sticks that killed
	with noise and fire.

They seemed to think the
	land was theirs, although
	they were so few,
They said it was un trés grand
	chasse de cerfs et
	caribous.

They gave the Indians knives
	and beads to paddle,
	portage, guide
Along the maze of waterways,
	exploring far and wide.

*New sights and sounds emerged
along the trails.*

The white man valued furs
and hides; the Indian,
blades of steel,
And so they traded knife or
axe for hunting skill and
zeal.

Then the fisher, marten,
beaver felt the steel trap's
vicious jaws,
And the Indian passed for
ever from the simple life
that was.

But the space was vast,
prolific, wherein a few
men ranged,
So, for all their craft and
effort, the land was little
changed.

---

*Winter travel throughout the park
was often done under trying
conditions.*

A hundred years went slowly
     by, and then a hundred
     more,
With very little to record or
     add to history's lore.

Except that men from other
     lands were slowly settling
     near,
And towns and farms and
     lumber mills came closer
     year by year.

Then there arose throughout
     the world a great demand
     for wood,
And timber cruisers searched
     this land and found that
     it was good.

*Lumbering probably reached its'
peak by the late 1800's.*

Then the brooding winter
　　silence was shattered by
　　the sound
Of thudding axe on pine trees
　　that went crashing to the
　　ground.

The work of felling giant trees
　　went on throughout the
　　day,
And the hewer with his broad
　　axe squared the timbers
　　as they lay.

In great gashes in the forest
　　all is tumult, disarray,
As men and horses labour to
　　drag the logs away.

Fellin' pine in Algonquin.

At night the tired men return
to where their comforts
lie,
The log camboose with
central fire beneath the
open sky.

Around the fire on looping
ropes, wet clothes are
slung on high,
Where, steaming in the heat
and smoke, they very
quickly dry.

The cook rules here, his word
is law, for none would
dare to cross
The guardian of the salted
pork, the undisputed
boss.

*The workers were housed in shanties
about 40 feet square, constructed
of logs dovetailed together and
chinked with moss and mud.*

Each man collects his plate
      and mug, and lines up for
      his share
Of pork and beans - or beans
      and pork - a most
      recurrent fare.

He also gets some scalding
      tea and quickly finds his
      place,
And eats his meal without a
      word, as if it were a race.

Far from the world's
      distractions as any
      cloistered monk,
He finds repose for weary
      limbs in rough and
      narrow bunk.

---

*The cook and cookee made all the
difference in so far as the morale of
workers in the camp.*

Led the idle, rich, and
        pampered toss in their
        sleepless beds,
The woodsman sleeps in
        blissful peace denied to
        crowned heads.

Breakfast is eaten in the dusk,
        for there must be no
        delay
In felling, trimming,
        squaring, throughout the
        winter day.

When warming spring
        approaches and the ice
        breaks up in May,
The swollen rivers rampage
        and float the logs away.

---

*Saturday night in a camboose
        camp.*

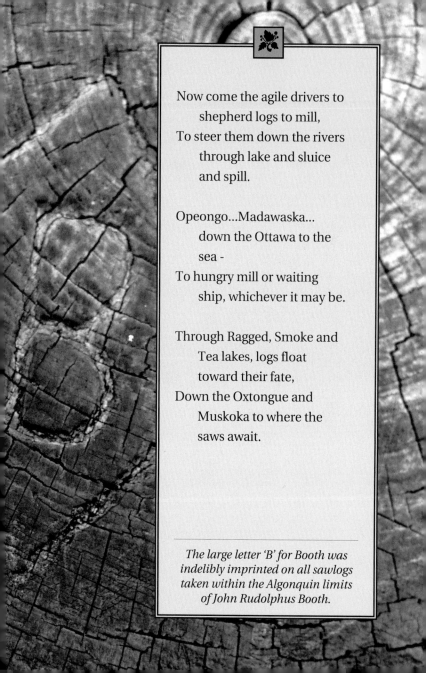

Now come the agile drivers to
shepherd logs to mill,
To steer them down the rivers
through lake and sluice
and spill.

Opeongo...Madawaska...
down the Ottawa to the
sea -
To hungry mill or waiting
ship, whichever it may be.

Through Ragged, Smoke and
Tea lakes, logs float
toward their fate,
Down the Oxtongue and
Muskoka to where the
saws await.

*The large letter 'B' for Booth was
indelibly imprinted on all sawlogs
taken within the Algonquin limits
of John Rudolphus Booth.*

Men work in constant danger
on rapids, chute and
dam,
Or riding heaving monsters
gyrating in a jam.

Hardy and brave were the
drivers, daring of limb
and life,
And many a lad returned no
more to his sweetheart or
his wife.

Down the great chute from
Porcupine was one man's
fatal ride,
And others rest in lonely
graves by the rapids
where they died.

*River drivers were a familiar sight
once the Spring break-up occurred.*

Gone are the river drivers,
    their skill not needed
    now,
For logs are moved in newer
    ways; to progress all must
    bow.

For time moves on and
    nothing stays, and soon
    the new is old,
Past days give place to other
    ways, just as a tale is told.

New methods speeded up
    the work, new logging
    roads were made,
Then came the fiery iron
    horse and railway lines
    were laid.

*The railroad running through the
Algonquin wilderness made the
park accessible to all. A group
comprising of officials of the J.R.
Booth Company Limited are shown
in this vintage photograph.*

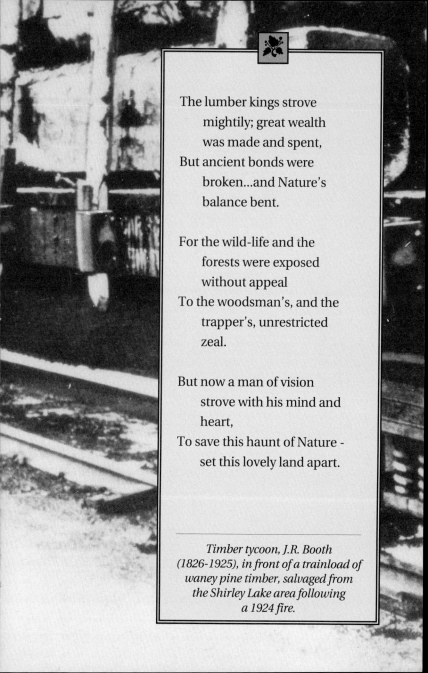

The lumber kings strove
    mightily; great wealth
    was made and spent,
But ancient bonds were
    broken...and Nature's
    balance bent.

For the wild-life and the
    forests were exposed
    without appeal
To the woodsman's, and the
    trapper's, unrestricted
    zeal.

But now a man of vision
    strove with his mind and
    heart,
To save this haunt of Nature -
    set this lovely land apart.

*Timber tycoon, J.R. Booth
(1826-1925), in front of a trainload of
waney pine timber, salvaged from
the Shirley Lake area following
a 1924 fire.*

Thus Alexander Kirkwood in
time achieved his mark,
and the highlands of Algonquin
became
Algonquin Park.

New policies of management
then came into effect,
And Nature and her workings
were treated with respect.

And Park became a sanctuary
for all within its fold;
And trapping was prohibited
and lumbering controlled.

Rangers were appointed and
stationed here and there
To uphold the regulations in
the regions in their care.

Mule deer.

Prohibition notwithstanding,
    trappers tried to keep
    their lines,
Using furtiveness and
    cunning to avoid arrest or
    fines.
But the efforts of the rangers
    made the risk so very
    great
That poaching quickly came
    to naught - or near at any
    rate.

Fire prevention and
    suppression received a
    welcome boost;
men were trained,
    equipment bought, and
    losses much reduced.

Hunter's cabin, circa 1897.

About this time the brothers
Wright perfected their
invention
That lifted man above the
earth, gave mind and
sight extension.

As guardian of the forest, the
aircraft soon proved best,
And by its means fires quickly
were located and
suppressed.

Thus came into existence a
piece of Earth apart,
A place of quiet beauty to
refresh the mind and
heart.

*The patrolling of Algonquin Park by
aircraft began in the early 1920's.*

Where water, woods and
    wild-life all bask in
    nature's smile,
Where every prospect
    pleases, and man dare
    not defile.

Far from the city's turmoil
    where Strife and Envy
    sway,
A sanctuary - a refuge - with
    nothing to dismay.

Artists, anglers, naturalists all
    found fulfillment here,
And the Park became a
    magnet that drew from
    far and near -

Bunch Berry.

All those who love the Out-
Of-Doors; all those with
the ability
To comprehend its peace and
joy, its beauty and
tranquility.

One artist caught the
radiance that on these
woodlands fell;
Tom Thomson showed us
magic and held us in its
spell.

And the beauty of his
painting for ever will
abide
In scenes of autumn glory by
Canoe Lake where he
died.

Tom Thomson.

*Veteran Canadian photographer,
Bob Muckleston, captured this
silhouette of a white pine tree,
during a 1953 photographic journey
throughout the interior of the park.*

A road was soon established
which ran from west to
east,
So all would come, enjoy the
Park, or part of it at least.

Then camps were instituted
where boys and girls were
taught
To value healthy outdoor
skills, and things that
can't be bought.

Research was undertaken in
the field of Park biology,
In forestry and fisheries, and
general ecology.

The west gate entrance in 1963.

Canoe routes were provided,
     the interior to span,
For those who wished to
     penetrate beyond the
     haunts of man -

Routes that led through
     chains of lakes, by rocky
     shores and islands,
With portage trails to pack
     across the piney-scented
     highlands.

Anglers in great numbers
     sought these waters fresh
     and pure
To try their skill with rod and
     line, and cunning bait
     and lure.

*Angling in Algonquin's lakes and
rivers has always been one of the
park's major attractions.*

To help them on their travels,
    local woodsmen found
    employ
To act as guides, to paddle,
    pack, or otherwise
    convoy -

As skillful cooks, camp-
    makers; and good
    companions who,
In every situation, knew
    exactly what to do.

Time, like an ever flowing
    stream, bears many
    things away,
And men and landmarks,
    once well known, no
    longer are today.

*American industrialist, George B.
Hayes and his associates, were early
park visitors. Unidentified native
guides are shown in this 1897 photo.*

The camboose camps are
gone now, their place all
but unknown,
New growth obscures their
rotting logs with verdant
moss o'er grown.

The shanty men are gone too,
gone like the winter's
snow,
Their monuments the great
pine stumps marked by
the axe's blow.

And many a guide with all his
skill and fund of
woodland lore,
Makes camp no more on
sylvan strand, as oft he
did of yore.

*Remains of old Algonquin Park
School. Local pupils included
John Wesley Dafoe, later to become
famous as Winnipeg Free Press
editor, journalist and
human rights crusader.*

The railway tracks have
    disappeared; the hostels
    are no more,
And in their place are trailer
    camps along the sandy
    shore.

But still the forest beckons,
    and still the lakes are
    blue,
And the joy and peace of
    nature is still forever new.

And the paddle and the
    tump-line will take you to
    the heart
Of placid, primal Nature - a
    peaceful world apart.

Old dam in the park, circa 1897.

If you paddle by the shore-
    line or walk along the trail
With an eye and ear for
    beauty, there's reward
    that will not fail.

You may see the purple
    violets, or the white
    arbutus flower;
Enchanting woodland
    scenery that changes
    every hour.

You may hear the wild wind
    sighing, as the lofty pine
    it sways,
And the rippling of the water
    where the dazzling
    sunlight plays.

Park Ranger, Ed Godin,
canoeing in Algonquin.

You may see the lowly
    dogwood with its scarlet
    berries ripe,
or the pretty little twin-flower,
    or the pallid Indian pipe.

You will hear the notes of bird
    song from shady tree and
    bush,
And the sweet celestial music
    of the hidden hermit
    thrush.

You may see the busy beaver,
    or the graceful white-
    tailed deer;
And the bear, racoon or otter,
    mink or marten may
    appear.

Chickadee.

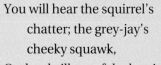

You will hear the squirrel's
    chatter; the grey-jay's
    cheeky squawk,
Or the shrill cry of the herring
    gull, alighting on a rock.

You may see the great moose
    wading in a lily-spangled
    bay,
Or the patient heron
    standing - watching for
    his prey.

Then across the lake at
    evening comes the
    laughter of the loon,
And through out the night,
    the great barred owl pays
    homage to the moon.

Common Loon.

This, then, is Algonquin Park,
    its history, purpose,
    beauty;
Its basic values to preserve, is
    now our bounden duty.

James Savage
    Smoke Lake
    Algonquin Park

Tea Lake Dam, July 1958.

Black Bear

Snowy Owl

Raccoon

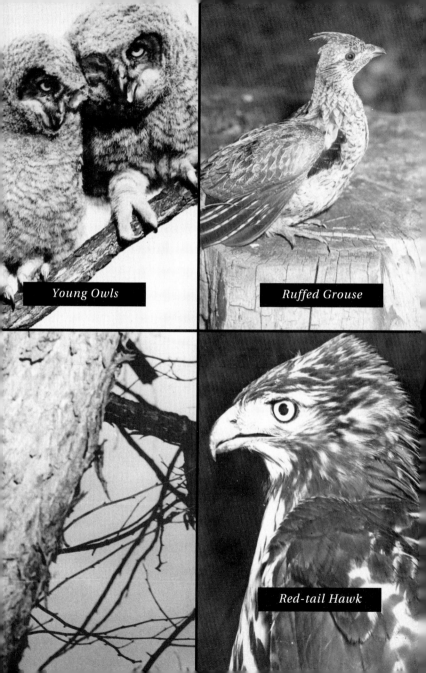

Young Owls

Ruffed Grouse

Red-tail Hawk

THE AUTHOR

James Savage is one of the comparatively small band of ecological pioneers whose early warnings are now bearing fruit in today's concern for the environment. He has made an outstanding contribution to the work of conservation education and is the recipient of numerous awards for his achievements as scientist and teacher. Mr. Savage taught at Neuchatel College, Switzerland and has served as a consultant in East Africa. He has written and edited a number of scientific books, articles and research papers. His book "Resources for Tomorrow" has made ecology meaningful for a whole generation of students.

James Savage has been a friend of Algonquin Park for most of a lifetime and is committed to promoting the ideals of its founders.

FOR FURTHER READING ABOUT ALGONQUIN PARK HISTORY,
WE RECOMMEND THE FOLLOWING BOOKS:

Tom Thomson, Blodwen Davies, Mitchell Press 1967

Tom Thomson - The Algonquin Years, Ottelyn Addison with
    Elizabeth Harwood, The Ryerson Press 1969

Early Days in Algonquin Park, Ottelyn Addison, McGraw-Hill
    Ryerson 1974

A Hundred Years A-Fellin', Charlotte Whitton, The Runge Press
    1974

Early Days in Haliburton, H.R. Cummings, Ontario Department
    of Lands and Forests 1962

The Upper Ottawa Valley, Clyde C. Kennedy, Renfrew County
    Council 1970

Along the Trail; With Ralph Bice in Algonquin Park, Natural
    Heritage/Natural History Inc. 1980

*Glimpses of Algonquin; Thirty Personal Impressions from Earliest
    Times to the Present*, G.D. Garland, The Friends of
    Algonquin Park 1989

A Pictorial History of Algonquin Provincial Park, Ministry of
    Natural Resources 1977

Fur; The Trade that Put Upper Canada on the Map, Ralph Bice,
    Ontario Trappers Association 1983

Taylor Statten; A Biography, C.A.M. Edwards, The Ryerson Press-
    Toronto 1960

ACKNOWLEDGEMENTS

The Publishers gratefully acknowledge the interest, courtesies and cooperation of the following: Isabelle Hambleton, Canadiana Department, Royal Ontario Museum; Sandy Cooke, Registrar, McMichael Canadian Art Collection; Irene Blogg Crich and, Michael Smart, Geographical Name Coordinator, Ministry of Natural Resources, Executive Secretary Ontario Geographic Names Board.

PHOTOGRAPHIC CREDITS

Outside Front Cover: McMichael Canadian Art Collection, #1975.22

Inside Front Cover: Ministry of Natural Resources

Page 6   Canadian National Railway Algonquin Park map, circa 1930. From the map library of the Ontario Geographic Names Board Secretariat

Page 8   Archives of Ontario, Acc 11611#7 SIG814

Page 10   Ministry of Natural Resources

Page 12   Royal Ontario Museum, #67 Can 140

Page 14   Royal Ontario Museum, #77 Can 487

Page 16   H.P.Sharp, Collection of the Publisher

Page 18   Ministry of Natural Resources, Bob Mucklestone, Photographer

Page 20   Ministry of Natural Resources

Page 22   National Archives of Canada

Page 24   Ministry of Natural Resources

Page 26   Ministry of Natural Resources

Page 28   Collection of the Publisher

Page 30   Ministry of Natural Resources, Cees Van, Photographer

Page 32   Archives of Ontario, Acc. 10847, Pt."1" #9

Page 34   Parks Historical #109-113

Page 36   Collection of the Publisher

Page 38   W. Victor Crich, F.R.P.S.

Page 40   Parks Historical #97-6

Page 42   Archives of Ontario, Acc. 12566-13

Page 44   W. Victor Crich, F.R.P.S.

Page 46   Archives of Ontario, Acc S2794

Page 47   Ministry of Natural Resources, Bob Mucklestone, Photographer

Page 48   Ministry of Natural Resources, Ted Jenkins, Photographer

Page 50   Ministry of Natural Resources

Page 52   Parks Historical, #97-2

Page 54   Archives of Ontario, Acc. 10106, Collection of the Publisher

Page 56   Parks Historical, #97-10

Page 58   Ministry of Natural Resources

Page 60   W. Victor Crich, F.R.P.S.

Page 62   W. Victor Crich, F.R.P.S.

Page 64   Ministry of Natural Resources, W. Masters, Photographer

Page 66   W. Victor Crich, F.R.P.S.

Inside Back Cover: Ministry of Natural Resources

ALGONQUIN

The park took its name from the Algonquins who excelled most of the Indian tribes in arts and other attainments. By the Iroquois they were called Adirondacks, that is "bark-eaters", in derision. In sober Indian they were called Odis qua gume, that is "people at the end of the water". They are supposed to have been at the head of a northern confederacy and to have descended the Ottawa at the close of the 10th century and to have occupied the left bank of the St. Lawrence. This family of Indians received the generic name Algonquins from the Algomequin, meaning "those on the other side", but now generally believed to be derived from the Micmac Algomaking, meaning "at the place of spearing fish".

From the origin and meaning of Place Names in Canada by
G.H. Armstrong. The MacMillan Company of Canada Limited, 1930.